About the Author™

Meet
E. B. White

S. Ward

The Rosen Publishing Group's
PowerKids Press™
New York

Published in 2001 by The Rosen Publishing Group, Inc.
29 East 21st Street, New York, NY 10010

First Edition

Book Design: Maria Melendez

Photo Credits: Cover, title page, pp. 2, 3, 4, 23 © The Everett Collection; p. 6 © International Stock; pp. 7, 8, 11, 16 © Bettmann/CORBIS; p. 15 © Yann Arthus-Bertrand/CORBIS; p. 12 © SuperStock; p. 13 © Archive Photos.

Grateful acknowledgment is made for permission to eprint previously published material on pp. 5, 18, 19, 20, 21, and 22: from STUART LITTLE by E. B. White, Stuart Little Collector's Edition, pictures by Garth Williams, watercolors of Garth Williams artwork by Rosemary Wells, copyright © 1945, by E. B. White; text copyright © renewed 1973 by E. B. White; illustrations copyright © renewed 1973 by Garth Williams; colorizations copyright © 1999 by Estate of Garth Williams; CHARLOTTE'S WEB by E. B. White, pictures by Garth Williams, copyright 1952 by E. B. White; text copyright © renewed 1980 by E. B. White; illustrations copyright © renewed 1980 by Estate of Garth Williams; CHARLOTTE'S WEB is a HarperTrophy paperback, a registered trademark of HarperCollins Publishers, Inc.; published by arrangement with HarperCollins Children's Books, a division of HarperCollins Publishers, and used with permission by HarperCollins Publishers, 10 East 53rd Street, New York, NY 10022.

Ward, S. (Stasia), 1968–
      Meet E. B. White / S. Ward.—1st ed.
         p. cm. — (About the author)
      Includes index.
      Summary: A simple biography of the multitalented author who wrote
the well-known children's books, "Charlotte's Web" and "Stuart Little."
      ISBN 0-8239-5713-6 (alk. paper)
      1. White, E. B. (Elwyn Brooks), 1899—Juvenile literature.
2. Authors, American—20th century—Biography—Juvenile literature.
[1. White, E. B. (Elwyn Brooks), 1899– 2. Authors, American.] I. Title.
II. Series.

PS3545.H5187 Z95 2001
818'.5209—dc21
[B]   00-025376

Manufactured in the United States of America

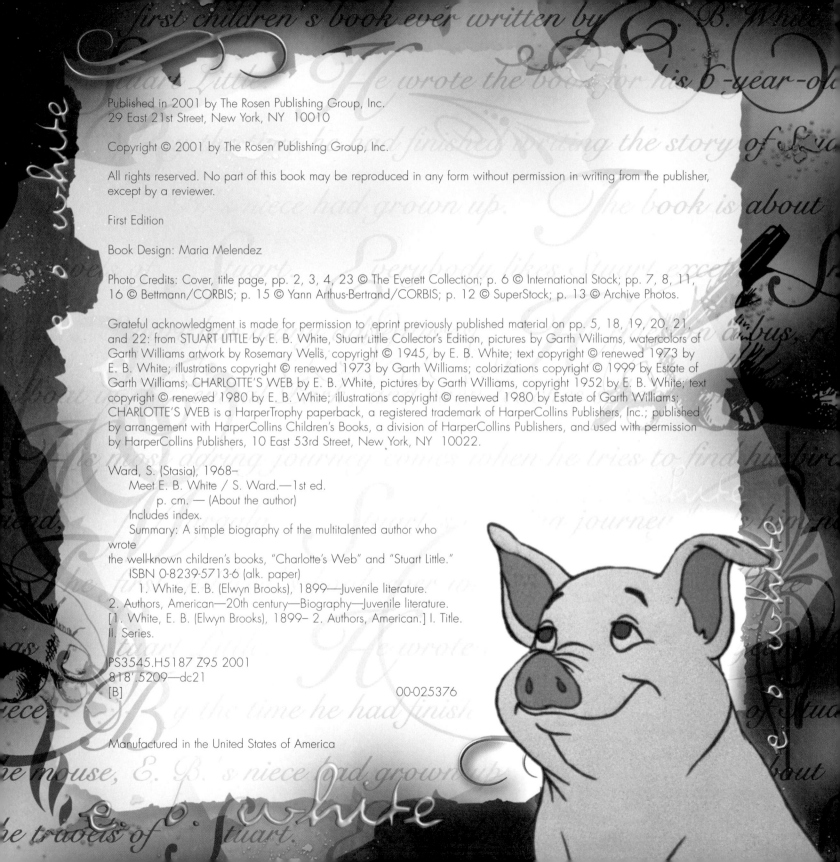

Contents

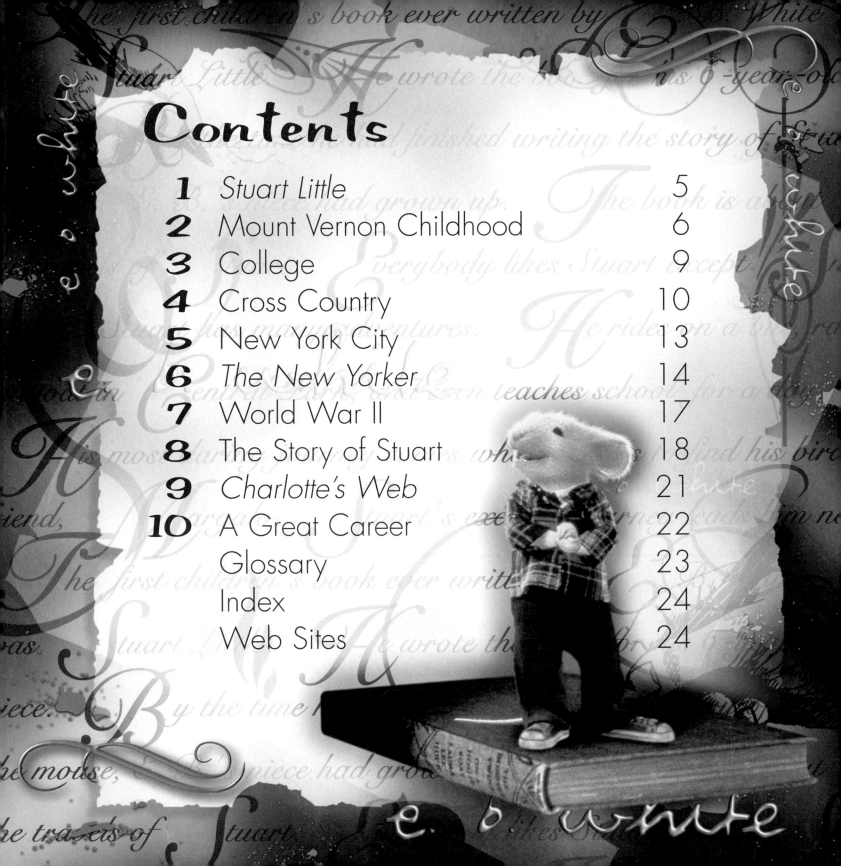

e. b. white

Stuart Little

In 1945, an **unusual** children's book was **published** by Harper & Brothers. The book was about a tiny mouse that was part of a human family. The mouse was named Stuart Little. The title of the book was also *Stuart Little*.

The **author** of *Stuart Little* was a man named E. B. White. E. B. White had been a well-known writer for adults for many years. At the age of 46, he became one of America's best-loved and best-selling children's book authors.

> "Stuart never paid any fare on buses, because he wasn't big enough to carry an ordinary dime. The only time he had . . ., he had rolled the coin along like a hoop . . .; but it had got away from him on a hill and had been snatched up by an old woman with no teeth."
>
> —from p. 29 of *Stuart Little* (1945)

◀ *Elwyn Brooks White used the name E. B. White when he wrote his books.*

Mount Vernon Childhood

Elwyn Brooks White was born on July 11, 1899. His father, Samuel, was a businessman. His mother, Jessie, took care of the family home in Mount Vernon, New York. Elwyn was their youngest child. He had five older brothers and sisters.

Elwyn did not like school very much. He was shy. He worried about speaking in front of the class. Elwyn loved nature. He loved to paddle a canoe. He liked to ice-skate on frozen ponds. He also loved to visit the zoo. He enjoyed learning about plants and animals.

This is a view of Fourth Avenue in Mount Vernon, New York, around 1910. Elwyn grew up in Mount Vernon. ▶

book ever written by

the book for his 6-y...

ory of Stua...

excepti...

white

he mouse, E. B.'s niece had grown up.

he travels of Stuart. Everybody...

e. b. white

College

After high school, Elwyn attended Cornell University in Ithaca, New York. He worked on the student newspaper, *The Cornell Daily Sun*. His writing was so good that he soon served as an **editor** of the *Sun*. Some of Elwyn's friends on the *Sun* gave him the **nickname** Andy. Elwyn would be called Andy for the rest of his life.

Andy became a member of the Manuscript Club. This club was a group of students who met each month to talk about writing. On Monday nights, Andy went to the home of Professor Bristow Adams to drink cocoa and talk about interesting subjects and ideas.

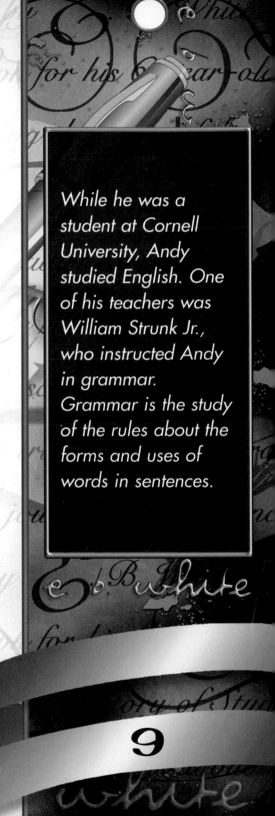

While he was a student at Cornell University, Andy studied English. One of his teachers was William Strunk Jr., who instructed Andy in grammar. Grammar is the study of the rules about the forms and uses of words in sentences.

Andy went to college at Cornell University in ◄ Ithaca, New York. He earned a diploma in English in 1921.

9

Cross Country

Andy and his friend Howard Cushman drove west across the United States after they graduated from college. They wrote about their experiences to get some practice in writing. They finally ended up living in Seattle, Washington, for a while.

After college Andy tried to get a job in New York City. He wanted to be a writer. He got a job as a newspaper **reporter**, but he was not very good at it. Reporting was not the kind of writing Andy wanted to do.

Andy grew tired of trying to find fun writing work in New York. In 1921, he and his friend Howard Cushman packed up Andy's Model T Ford car and started driving out west. They had a great adventure. When they ran out of money, they took jobs to pay for gas and food. They wrote stories about their trip. Andy sometimes made money selling his stories to newspapers.

Andy and a friend drove an old Model T, probably like the one shown here, out west. They liked the idea of being free to go and to do whatever they wanted.

book ever written by

wrote the book for his 6-y

the mouse, E. B.'s niece had grown up.

the travels of Stuart

white

e. b. white

New York City

Andy got a newspaper job in Seattle, Washington, but not as a reporter. He wrote short, funny stories. He wrote his opinions about things that happened in the world. Still he was not much of a success as a writer. He left his job and got work on a trading ship. In 1924, after the boat trip ended, Andy returned to New York.

In New York City, Andy got a job writing for an **advertising agency**. He also wrote poems. Some of his writing was published in *The Conning Tower*. This magazine printed poems and stories by some of the leading writers of the day.

This picture shows a busy street in New York City during the 1920s. Andy's writing began to be noticed by people around 1925, when his work was printed in a leading New York magazine.

A nighttime view of New York City.

13

The New Yorker

While Andy was writing for The New Yorker, he met an editor there. Her name was Katharine Angell. On November 13, 1929, Andy and Katharine got married. Andy became a stepfather to Katharine's two children. The following year, Andy and Katharine welcomed a new addition to their family, a son.

In February 1925, a new magazine appeared in New York City. It was called *The New Yorker*. It was different from any other magazine being printed at the time. It hired very good writers and the people working there had a sense of what was smart and fun. Andy sent an **essay** to the magazine. The magazine printed it. Soon Andy had a job writing for *The New Yorker*. His writing helped make *The New Yorker* a success. *The New Yorker* was important to Andy for another reason. He met Katharine Angell there. Andy and Katharine fell in love and got married.

Andy got a full-time job at The New Yorker magazine in 1927. The magazine was located ▶ in New York City in the building shown here.

BOMBERS RAID MANILA

IN THE NEWS

WELL, fellow Americans, we are in the war and we have got to win it.

There may have been some difference of opinion among good Americans about getting into the war, but there is no difference about how we should come out of it.

We must come out victorious and with the largest V in the alphabet.

We are not completely prepared for war.

We have not got a Swiss system of universal service that we will have to have some day, since the lands are full of robbers and sea of pirates.

But we will get better and stronger every day, and we will not have to get very good and very strong to knock the everlasting daylights out of Japan.

We may have some small reverses at first, but do not let that worry you—if it happens.

It is not who wins the first round, but who wins the last one that counts for victory.

And there is no doubt about the victory, folks—none whatever.

The worst thing about the war with Japan is that it will divide our efforts and prevent us from rendering all out aid to England if we were doing and wanting further to do.

But we will still manage to keep Britain going with our right hand while we poke Japan in the nose with our left.

Japan has been wanting war for a long time.

It has been swaggering around Asia, murdering a lot of unarmed Chinamen.

Now it is going to get a war and a real one.

Fortunately we are well on our way towards a dominating and determining two ocean navy and an all skies aeroplane fleet.

Fortunately we can manufacture ten ships to Japan's one, and ten aeroplanes to Japan's one.

Naturally we can fly the skies better and fight the Japs better.

And that means that as soon as we swing into action we will wash up the war.

Japan's attack on Hawaii is probably with the idea of keeping us on defense at home.

But we will not stay at home and we will not stay on defense.

Before the war is over we will have burned up all the paper houses in Japan and sunk most of their scrap iron battleships and put this bunch of Oriental marauders back on the right little, tight little, out-of-sight little island where they belong.

And we will have fenced them in there.

Then maybe we will let them have a little bit—coal to operate if we cannot help it set.

Our main concern now is

U. S. DECLARES WAR ON JAPAN

Journal ⟨NEW YORK⟩ American

B | ⟨AN AMERICAN PAPER FOR THE AMERICAN PEOPLE⟩ | In Two Sections—Section One | 5¢

No. 19,707—DAILY | MONDAY, DECEMBER 8, 1941 | DAILY | SATURDAY | SUNDAY
3 Cents | 5 Cents | 10 Cents

7TH SPORT
★★★★★
WALL ST. CLOSING

The President's Message

WASHINGTON, Dec. 8 (UP) — Following is the text of President Roosevelt's message to Congress today asking for the declaration of war:

"To the Congress of the United States:

Yesterday, Dec. 7, 1941 — a date which will live in infamy — the United States of America was suddenly and deliberately attacked by naval and air forces of the Empire of Japan.

"The United States was at peace with that nation and, at the solicitation of Japan, was still in conversation with its Government and its Emperor looking toward the maintenance of peace in the Pacific.

"Indeed, one hour after Japanese air squadrons had commenced bombing in Oahu, the Japanese Ambassador to the United States and his colleague delivered to the Secretary of State a formal reply to a recent American message.

"While this reply stated that is seemed useless to continue the existing diplomatic negotiations, it contained no threat or hint of war or armed attack.

"It will be recorded that the distance of Hawaii from Japan makes it obvious that the attack was deliberately planned many days or even weeks ago.

"During the intervening time the Japanese Government has deliberately sought to deceive the United States by false statements and expressions of hope for continued peace.

Many American Lives Lost

"The attack yesterday on the Hawaiian Islands has caused severe damage to American naval and military forces. Very many American lives have been lost. In addition American ships have been reported torpedoed on the high ⟨seas⟩ between San Francisco and Honolulu.

"Yesterday ⟨the Japanese⟩ Government also launched an ⟨attack⟩

"Last night Japanese forces attacked the Philippine Islands.

"Last night Japanese forces attacked Wake Island.

This morning the Japanese attacked Midway Island.

Will Win Through

"Japan has, therefore, undertaken a surprise offensive extending throughout the Pacific area. The acts of yesterday speak for themselves. The people of the United States have already formed their opinions and well understand the implications to the very life and safety of our nation.

"As Commander-in-Chief of the Army and Navy I have directed that all measures be taken for our defense.

"Always will we remember the character of the onslaught against us.

"No matter how long it may take us to overcome this premeditated invasion, the American people in their righteous might will win through to absolute victory.

"I believe I interpret the will of the Congress and of the people when I assert that we will not only defend ourselves to the uttermost but will make very certain that this form of treachery shall never endanger us again.

"Hostilities exist. There is no blinking at the fact that our people, our territory and our interests are in grave danger.

"With confidence in our armed forces — with the unbounding determination of our people — we will gain the inevitable triumph — So help us God.

"I ask that the Congress declare that since the unprovoked attack by Japan on Sunday, December 7th, a state of war existed between the United States and the Japanese Empire."

WASHINGTON, Dec. 8 (UP). — Congress today proclaimed existence of a state of war between the United States and the Japanese Empire 33 minutes after the dramatic moment when President Roosevelt stood before a joint session to pledge that we will triumph — "so help us, God."

The Senate acted first, adopting the resolution by a unanimous roll call vote of 82 to 0, within 21 minutes after the President had concluded his address to a joint session of both Houses.

The House voted immediately afterward.

The final House vote was announced as 388 to 1. The lone negative vote was cast by Rep. Jeannette Rankin (R.-Mont.), who also voted against entry into World War I.

Hisses Greet Vote

The resolutions were before both Houses within fifteen minutes of the time Mr. Roosevelt ended his seven-minute, 500-word extraordinary message.

There was a half second of uncertainty ⟨in the⟩ House when Rep. Jannette Rankin (R.-Mont.) ⟨…⟩

Continued on Page A Column 1

War At A Glance

The United States declared war on Japan today.

America's battle fleet swung into action against Japan, aided by the British and Australians.

White House statements said a number of Japanese planes and submarines already had been destroyed. There were reports of a naval battle off the Philippines.

Japan's bombing of Hawaii cost the U. S. 1,500 lives, one battleship, a destroyer and many planes, the White House said, but declared the fight was continuing.

Japan attacked Guam, Wake and Midway Islands, the Philippines, Hongkong, Tientsin and

1,500 U. S. Dead In Hawaii Rai⟨d⟩

⟨…⟩ Dec. 8 (UP)

World War II

Andy was a nervous man. He worried about his health. He worried about his writing. He worried that the world was getting closer and closer to another war. He worried about how hard it was to live in New York City.

In 1937, Andy quit *The New Yorker* and moved with his family to a farm in North Brooklin, Maine. He started writing a column called "One Man's Meat," for *Harper's* magazine. By the end of 1941, the United States had started fighting in World War II. Andy decided to move back to New York and to write again for *The New Yorker*.

In 1937, Andy and Katharine bought a farm in Maine. Andy loved living and working on the farm. His love of nature made him care a lot about the world around him. He believed that people around the world should take care of all living things and their surroundings.

The front page of this newspaper announces the United States's entry into World War II. The country declared war on Japan on December 8, 1941.

The Story of Stuart

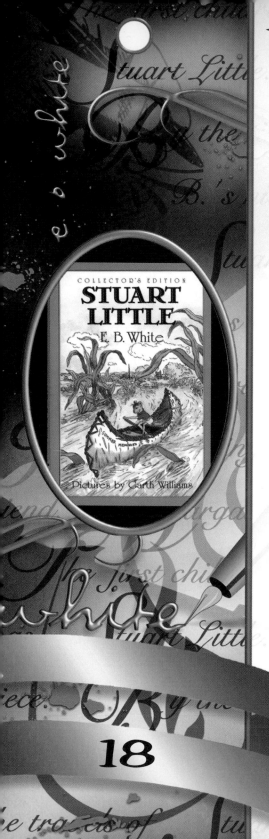

After the war, Andy did not want to keep working full time at *The New Yorker*. Years earlier he had started to write stories about a little mouse named Stuart Little. Now he wanted to finish the stories. In 1945, *Stuart Little* was published. Stuart is a mouse who is born into a human family. Stuart is small, but he also is brave and smart. At the end of the story, Stuart leaves home to look for a bird named Margalo, his lost love. This ending left some children and grown-ups with questions about Stuart and Margalo, but Andy thought the ending was just right. It showed that life is not always easy to understand.

This is a picture from Stuart Little *showing Stuart spraying himself with his mother's perfume. Stuart had to take a shower because he got slimy after going down the bathtub drain.* ▶

Charlotte's Web

In 1949, Andy began writing another book for children. This book was called *Charlotte's Web*. It is the story of an eight-year-old girl named Fern, a pig named Wilbur, and a smart spider named Charlotte. Charlotte saves Wilbur from being **slaughtered**, or killed, by writing words in her web. Everyone thinks Wilbur wrote the words. Wilbur becomes famous. People come to see the famous spelling pig. The family farm becomes famous, too. Fern's father decides to keep Wilbur for a pet instead of slaughtering him. Charlotte dies after saving Wilbur. He is sad but never forgets his good friend, Charlotte.

◀ *Charlotte lays eggs and dies after saving Wilbur. He is sad, but he is not lonely. Charlotte's spider children hatch in the spring to keep him company.*

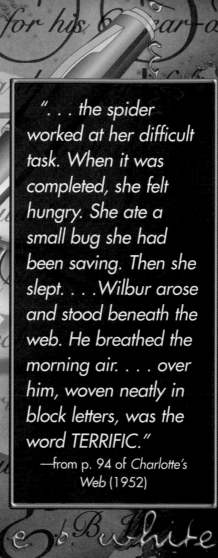

"... the spider worked at her difficult task. When it was completed, she felt hungry. She ate a small bug she had been saving. Then she slept. ...Wilbur arose and stood beneath the web. He breathed the morning air. ... over him, woven neatly in block letters, was the word TERRIFIC."
—from p. 94 of *Charlotte's Web* (1952)

21

A Great Career

In 1970, E. B. White wrote one more children's book. The book was called *The Trumpet of the Swan*. It was about a swan named Louis and a boy named Sam. E. B. White also kept writing for grown-ups. He collected his essays and letters and made them into books. He also cowrote a book about writing called *The Elements of Style* that is still used today.

E. B. White died on October 1, 1985, in North Brooklin, Maine. His books continue to touch the minds and hearts of readers around the world.

E. B. White received many honors, or prizes, for his great writing. These honors included the Presidential Medal of Freedom, the Laura Ingalls Wilder Award, the National Medal for Literature, and a Pulitzer Prize special citation, or recognition, for his writings.

Glossary

advertising agency (AD-vur-tyz-ing AY-jen-see) A business that tries to sell something by announcing it publicly.

author (AW-thur) A person who writes books, articles, or reports.

editor (EH-dih-ter) The person in charge of correcting errors, checking facts, and deciding what will be printed in a newspaper, book, or magazine.

essay (EH-say) A short piece of writing that looks at something from a personal point of view.

nickname (NIK-naym) A funny and interesting name that is used instead of a person's real name.

published (PUH-blisht) Something that is printed for people to read.

reporter (ree-POR-ter) A person who tells people the news.

slaughtered (SLAW-terd) When an animal has been killed for food.

unusual (un-YOO-zhoo-uhl) Different.

Index

Web Sites

To learn more about E. B. White, check out these Web sites:

http://11207.38.230.145/bw/author.asp?author=1086

http://www.Kirjasto.sci.fi/ebwhite.htm